Splashtime for Zoo Animals

by Caroline Arnold   **photographs by Richard Hewett**

Carolrhoda Books, Inc./Minneapolis

Splish, splash,
take a bath.
Zoo animals need
water every day.
They use it in many
different ways.

tiger

Penguins cannot fly,
but they are
super swimmers.

penguin

Killer whales spend
their whole lives
in the water.

killer whales

Sea lions play
in the waves.

sea lions

Two polar bears
use their pool
as a boxing ring.

polar bears

Elk keep cool in the water on a hot summer day.

elk

One baby swan gets
a ride, while the other
one swims.

swans

Most frogs need
water to keep their
skin moist.

frogs

A crested crane
searches for food
in the water.

crested crane

Two tigers toss a
ball in the water.

tigers

A lizard dips its tongue into the water for a drink.

lizard

A snow leopard slips
and makes a splash.

snow leopard

A young panda takes
a dip to cool off.

panda

Animals cannot live without water. Neither can you.

elephant

Where can I find...

hippopotamuses

Caroline Arnold has written more than one hundred books for children. Many of the books are about animals. Caroline lives with her husband in Los Angeles, California.

Richard Hewett worked for magazines before he discovered children's books. He, too, has created many books about animals. Richard lives with his wife in Los Angeles, California.

Text copyright © 1999 by Caroline Arnold
Photographs copyright © 1999 by Richard R. Hewett
Additional photographs courtesy of: © Caroline Arnold, p. 21; © Arthur Arnold, pp. 11, 17, 23

This book is available in two bindings:
ISBN 1-57505-288-1 (lib. bdg.)
ISBN 1-57505-394-2 (trade bdg.)

Carolrhoda Books, Inc., c/o The Lerner Publishing Group
241 First Avenue North, Minneapolis, MN 55401 U.S.A.

Website address: www.lernerbooks.com

Library of Congress Cataloging-in-Publication Data

Arnold, Caroline.
   Splashtime for zoo animals / by Caroline Arnold ; photographs by Richard Hewett.
      p.   cm.
   Includes index.
   Summary: In text and photographs, describes the behavior of zoo animals
who live, take a drink, or play in the water.
   ISBN 1–57505–288–1 (lib. bdg. : alk. paper)
   1. Zoo animals—Water requirements—Juvenile literature. 2. Zoo animals—Behavior—
Juvenile literature. [1. Zoo animals. 2. Water.] I. Hewett, Richard, ill. II. Title.
QL77.5.A855   1999
636.088'9—dc21   98-24378

Manufactured in the United States of America
1 2 3 4 5 6 – JR – 04 03 02 01 00 99